TIMES) SERIES YOU CHOOSE

YOU CHOOSE™
BOOKS

THE CALIFORNIA GOLD RUSH

An Interactive History Adventure

by Elizabeth Raum

Consultant:
Malcolm Rohrbough, Professor of History
University of Iowa
Author, *Days of Gold: The California Gold Rush
and the American Nation*

Capstone
press®

Mankato, Minnesota

You Choose Books are published by Capstone Press,
151 Good Counsel Drive, P.O. Box 669, Mankato, Minnesota 56002.
www.capstonepress.com

Library of Congress Cataloging-in-Publication Data
Raum, Elizabeth.
 The California Gold Rush: an interactive history adventure / by Elizabeth Raum.
 p. cm.—(You choose books)
 Summary: "Describes the events of the nineteenth century California gold rush.
The reader's choices reveal historical details of how miners traveled, how they looked
for gold, and their impact on California's history"—Provided by publisher.
 Includes bibliographical references and index.
 ISBN-13: 978-1-4296-0160-3 (hardcover)
 ISBN-10: 1-4296-0160-4 (hardcover)
 ISBN-13: 978-1-4296-1179-4 (softcover pbk.)
 ISBN-10: 1-4296-1179-0 (softcover pbk.)
 1. California—Gold discoveries—Juvenile literature. 2. Frontier and pioneer
life—California—Juvenile literature. 3. California—History—1846–1850—Juvenile
literature. I. Title. II. Series.
F865.R285 2008
979.4'04—dc22   2007006223

Editorial Credits: Megan Schoeneberger, editor; Juliette Peters, designer; Laura Manthe
 and Wanda Winch, photo researchers

Photo Credits: The Bancroft Library, University of California, Berkeley, 26; The Bancroft
Library, University of California, Berkeley, "Incident on the Chagres River, Panama" by
Charles Christian Nahl, 20; The Bancroft Library, University of California, Berkeley,
Zelda Mackay Pictorial Collection, 78; The Bancroft Library, University of California,
Berkeley/Robert B. Honeyman, Jr. Collection of Early Californian and Western American
Pictorial Material, "The Way They Crossed the Isthmus" by Nathaniel Currier, image
altered, 31; California Historical Society, FN-04312, 98; Collection of Greg French, 91;
Corbis/Bettmann, 8, 12, 86, 100; Courtesy of the California History Room, California
State Library, Sacramento, California, cover, 84, 94; Historichwy49.com, 89; The Denver
Public Library/Western History Collection/Frenzeny & Tavernier, Call No. Z-3265, 64;
The Denver Public Library/Western History Collection/William Henry Jackson, Call
No. WHJ-10614, 48; Library of Congress, 105; The Long Island Museum of American
Art, History & Carriages. Gift of Mr. and Mrs. Ward Melville, 1955, 6; maps.com, 10,
42; Mary Evans Picture Library/Grosvenor Prints, 75; NOAA, 70; North Wind Picture
Archives, 17, 34, 38, 40, 54, 60, 103; Oregon Trail Museum Association, 51

102009
005614R

TABLE OF CONTENTS

ABOUT YOUR ADVENTURE

YOU are a New Englander with a bad case of gold fever. Gold has been discovered in California, and you want to go claim some for yourself. Will you strike it rich?

In this book, you'll explore how the choices people made meant the difference between wealth and poverty, even life and death. The events you'll experience happened to real people.

Chapter One sets the scene. Then you choose which path to read. Follow the directions at the bottom of each page. The choices you make will change your outcome. After you finish one path, go back and read the others for new perspectives and more adventures.

YOU CHOOSE the path you take through history.

People learned about the discovery of gold by reading articles in newspapers.

GOLD FEVER

"Listen to this," your father says, reading today's paper. "Two California gold miners made $17,000 in seven days. That's a fortune! If I were a young man . . ." he sighs.

Your mother smiles. She's pleased that your father is not rushing off to California and leaving her behind to watch the store and your younger brothers and sisters.

People everywhere have gold fever. You do too. On August 19, 1848, the *New York Herald* reported the discovery of gold in California. The news reached your local paper later that month. Ever since, you have dreamed of going west to collect riches for yourself.

7

Turn the page.

THE EMIGRANT'S GUIDE TO THE GOLD MINES.

THREE WEEKS

IN THE

GOLD MINES,

OR

ADVENTURES WITH THE GOLD DIGGERS OF CALIFORNIA

In August, 1848.

TOGETHER WITH

ADVICE TO EMIGRANTS,

WITH FULL INSTRUCTIONS UPON THE BEST METHOD OF GETTING
THERE, LIVING, EXPENSES, ETC., ETC., AND A

COMPLETE DESCRIPTION OF THE COUNTRY,

With a Map and Illustrations.

BY HENRY I. SIMPSON,

OF THE NEW YORK VOLUNTEERS.

NEW YORK:

JOYCE AND CO., 40 ANN STREET.

1848.

Guidebooks like this one offered advice to gold seekers.

"I am a young man," you remind your father. "And I'd like to take my chances in California. If only I could afford the trip."

"I'm happy to lend you money for the trip," your father says. "When you return with your pockets full of gold, you can repay the loan twice over."

"Go if you must," your mother says. "But I don't want you going to California by ship. Ships sink."

"I'll choose a ship without leaks," you say with a smile. "Ships are the safest way to reach California." You hand her your copy of *The Emigrant's Guide to the Gold Mines*. "Here, you can read it yourself. The trip is fast and easy."

Turn the page.

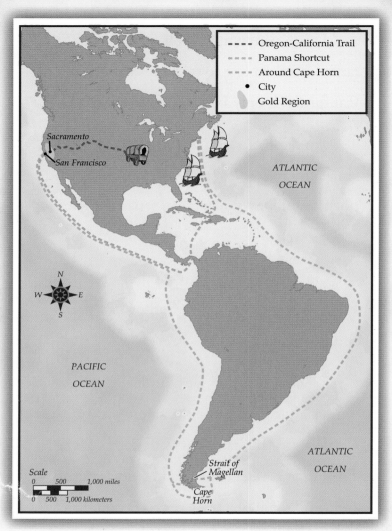

Oregon-California Trail
Panama Shortcut
Around Cape Horn
● City
Gold Region

Sacramento
San Francisco

ATLANTIC
OCEAN

N
W　E
S

PACIFIC
OCEAN

ATLANTIC
OCEAN

Strait of
Magellan
Cape
Horn

Scale
0   500   1,000 miles
0   500   1,000 kilometers

10

"If I were going to California," your father says, "I'd sign on with a wagon train and go overland. I like to keep solid ground beneath my feet. Imagine seeing this great land firsthand."

"That's a terrible idea," your mother says. "Crossing those rugged mountains and dry deserts is dangerous. You could die of thirst."

You laugh. "One way, there's too much water. The other, there's not enough. I promise to be careful. Next time you see me I'll be a rich man, and I'll have stories to last a lifetime."

Will they be stories of a journey by sea or by land?

➤ To go by sea, turn to page 13.

➤ To take the overland route, turn to page 41.

CALIFORNIA

AND THE

GOLD REGION DIRECT!

The Magnificent, Fast Sailing and favorite packet Ship,

JOSEPHINE,

BURTHEN 400 TONS, CAPT.

Built in the most *superb* manner of Live Oak, White Oak and Locust, for a New York and Liverpool Packet; thoroughly Copper-fastened and Coppered. She is a very fast sailer, having crossed the Atlantic from Liverpool to New-York in 14 days, the shortest passage ever made by a *Sailing Ship*. Has superior accommodations for Passengers, can take Gentlemen with their Ladies and families. Will probably reach ☞ SAN FRANCISCO **THIRTY DAYS** ahead of any Ship sailing at the same time. Will sail about the

10th November Next.

For Freight or Passage apply to the subscriber,

RODNEY FRENCH,

No. 103 North Water Street. Rodman's Wharf

New Bedford, October 15th.

Posters advertised ships heading to California.

CHAPTER 2

A SEA VOYAGE

As a child, you often pretended to sail to a magical island and dig for treasure. Now you are heading to California by ship in search of real gold. It's a dream come true.

Everyone who stops by your father's store is talking about the gold rush. When they hear that you'll be sailing to California soon, they are quick to offer advice.

"My friends and I will be sailing around South America for a safe trip to California," one man tells you. "We've started a company. Everyone pays $600. That covers the boat trip and a cargo of lumber, bricks, and eight ready-to-build houses."

Turn the page.

Your father nods. "I suppose that in a growing town like San Francisco, there will be a good market for building supplies."

"We believe so," the man continues. "When we get to San Francisco, we'll sell the cargo, and everyone will share the profits. Why don't you join us?"

A man leaning on the counter interrupts. "There's a better way to go—the shortcut through Panama. I'll be in California in six weeks. Your ship around South America could take six months."

"The shortcut may be fast, but it's dangerous," the first man says. "You'll have to sail to Chagres on Panama's eastern coast and then cross the jungle. If you make it through alive, you've still got to take one more boat to San Francisco."

"It's all arranged ahead of time," the second man says. "A bunk below deck on our steamship will cost you just $200. You're welcome to join us."

You consider both men's plans. The way around South America may seem safer, but it is also more costly. The Panama shortcut is cheaper and faster. But lots of things could go wrong in the jungle. Which do you choose?

➻ To sail around South America,
turn to page 16.

➻ To take the shortcut through Panama,
turn to page 19.

Your mother is pleased you've chosen the safer route around South America. Your father likes the company's plan to make money by selling its cargo in San Francisco.

You go to Boston, the nearest seaport, to board the *Golden Eagle*. The ship leaves Boston on January 16, 1849. At first, you stand on deck watching the waves pound the ship. But seasickness soon sends you to your bunk.

After a week, you move around the ship as easily as the sailors do. You make friends with fellow passengers—bricklayers, butchers, farmers, paper makers, carpenters, painters, lawyers, and store clerks.

Ships going to California were crowded with people, mostly men, hoping to strike it rich in the gold fields.

You sail for weeks and weeks. The harsh New England winter gives way to warmer tropical temperatures as you sail south. But as you approach Cape Horn, the weather turns cold again. Soon the captain will decide whether to go around the Horn or through the Strait of Magellan.

Turn the page.

Ships going around Cape Horn face waves 80 to 90 feet tall. Ice coats the ship, snapping masts in two. The remains of ships and cargoes line the shores.

But the strait is dangerous too. Sudden storms smash ships against the rocky coast. Thick fog hides dangers from view. Some ship captains claim that it is quicker to go through the strait, but others say it depends on the weather and the ship. Neither way is easy. Do you think the captain should go around Cape Horn or through the Strait of Magellan?

➻ To go around Cape Horn, turn to page 22.

➻ To go through the Strait of Magellan, turn to page 23.

To get to California quickly, you decide to take the shortcut through Panama. The steamship leaves Boston on January 16, 1849. Ten days later, you arrive in the village of Chagres, Panama's eastern port. Several ships have beaten you there, but your group has reserved rooms, canoes, and mules for the rest of the journey. Those who didn't plan ahead are stuck waiting.

At the hotel, you share space on the dirt floor with 25 others. At mealtime, a waiter asks, "Do you want monkey meat or iguana for dinner?"

"Nothing, thank you," you answer. You've lost your appetite.

Turn the page.

The next morning, you and three others begin the journey up the Chagres River in a dugout canoe called a bungo. As natives paddle you the 50 miles to Gorgona, monkeys chatter in the trees of the steamy rainforest.

Travelers hired natives to transport them up the Chagres River in boats called bungos.

As you approach Gorgona, the natives use poles to push the bungo through the strong currents. You offer to jump into the river and help pull the bungo along.

"Don't do it," one of the men says. "Not in this heat. You'll die of heat stroke."

"What if there are snakes?" says another.

You are anxious to reach the gold fields, and the bungo is moving slowly. With your help, the natives could push the bungo more quickly. The sooner you reach Gorgona, the sooner you'll get to California.

But the sun is very hot, and heat stroke is a real danger. Is saving a little time worth the risk?

➻ To help pull the bungo, turn to page **29**.

➻ To stay in the bungo, turn to page **31**.

The ship heads for Cape Horn. Huge winds rock the ship. It's impossible to stand on deck without holding onto something. Even some of the crew get seasick. There are barely enough sailors to keep up with repairs on the ship.

The first night, winds batter the ship so badly that one of the sails, the jib, comes loose. "Will anyone volunteer to fix it?" the captain asks. "Waiting for the crew to be healthy will delay our journey." No one steps forward. "It's easy," he says, "Just climb into the rigging and reattach the jib. Sailors do it all the time. Who will volunteer?"

Fixing the jib may be easy for a sailor. Will it be easy for you?

➤ *To volunteer, turn to page **38**.*

➤ *If you don't volunteer, turn to page **25**.*

After a night at anchor, the captain heads into the Strait of Magellan. Strong winds force him to turn back.

"We'll wait for the waves to die down," he says.

Days often begin pleasantly. The ship makes some progress, but the winds and high waves return. After 19 days, the ship is not quite halfway through the Strait.

Turn the page.

The captain stops for repairs at Port Famine in Chile on the north side of the Strait. Other ships are anchored beside you. You look over at the nearest ship, and a familiar face smiles back. "Neal Nye!" you shout. You went to school with Neal. What a surprise to see him here!

"Why not join me on the *Hackstaff*, my friend?" Neal says. "This ship is fast. We'll get to the gold first."

"I've already paid my passage on the *Golden Eagle*. I have no money left to buy passage on another ship."

"The captain is short of crew. Perhaps, if you're willing to work . . ."

➤ If you remain with the Golden Eagle, go to page **25**.

➤ To switch to the Hackstaff, turn to page **28**.

You're no sailor. Leave the work to them. You'd rather enjoy the trip as a passenger. Stopping for repairs means extra delays, but you're not worried. From what you've heard, there's plenty of gold to be found in California.

The dull days at sea drag on. The only decent meal is lobscouse, a hash made from potatoes, onions, salt meat, and dry bread. Twice a week you have duff, a pudding made from dried fruit, flour, and suet.

Turn the page.

Abandoned ships filled San Francisco Bay as more and more gold seekers came to California.

Finally, on July 9, 1849, the ship sails into San Francisco Bay through the narrow neck called the Golden Gate. Hundreds of ships have been left behind in the bay while their captains and crews search for gold.

It's tempting to go straight to the gold fields. The sooner you start digging, the sooner you'll be rich. But the company has supplies to sell, and part of the profit belongs to you. If you go directly to the gold fields, you might lose out on your share. On the other hand, will the profit matter once you find gold?

➤ To wait in San Francisco, turn to page **71**.

➤ To go to the gold fields, turn to page **77**.

The captain accepts your offer to work in exchange for passage on the *Hackstaff*. The ship is as fast as Neal promised, and you are soon through the Strait and heading for San Francisco.

Good winds and smooth sailing bring you to San Francisco Bay on June 25, 1849. Neal wants you to go directly to the gold fields with him. "The sooner we start digging, the sooner we'll be rich."

But maybe you should wait for your company to arrive. After all, when they sell their cargo, you'll have a share of the money. The plan was to meet them at the Parker House Hotel. Do you wait or not?

➤ To wait in San Francisco, turn to page 71.

➤ To go to the gold fields, turn to page 77.

You jump into the water and grab a rope. For several miles, you pull the bungo against the rushing water. Recent rains have swollen the river, causing strong currents. Finally, you see the city of Gorgona. "We made it!" you shout. But just as soon as the words are out of your mouth, you pass out and disappear beneath the water. One of the natives pulls you to land.

Turn the page.

A doctor traveling through Gorgona says you have heat stroke. He gives you water to cool you. When you begin to recover, he suggests that you return to Boston. "Cholera has killed many people in nearby villages. The heat stroke left you weak and more likely to catch this deadly disease."

You are halfway to California and the gold. You hate to turn back. But if your life depends on it . . .

To return to Boston, turn to page **33**.

To go on, turn to page **34**.

Your friends convince you to stay in the bungo. "Save all that energy for the gold fields."

The bungo arrives safely at Gorgona, a village of about 100 houses. Your group has arranged for a mule train to take you and your baggage 20 miles overland to Panama City.

At Gorgona, Panama, travelers switched to mules to carry them the rest of the way to Panama City.

Turn the page.

The trip by mule is not easy. Constant rain makes the trail as slick as an ice rink. One of the mules plunges down a bank into mud nearly 5 feet deep. It dies trapped in the mud. By the time you reach Panama City, you are a muddy mess.

"Where is the ship for San Francisco?" you ask.

The others in your company shake their heads. "The ship sailed without us. Here's your ticket. Take any ship you can find."

But you don't find many ships going to San Francisco. Those you do find are full. There are hundreds of people waiting to get to California.

Turn to page **36**.

Once you've made the difficult decision to return home, you feel relief. Your mother would never forgive you if you died of cholera.

You repeat the journey back across Panama, this time with a different group of travelers. As you lie in the boat, you think about all that you have lost: money you paid for passage, dreams of gold, and stories of adventure. Then you think about what you have saved—your life.

THE END

To follow another path, turn to page 11.
To read the conclusion, turn to page 101.

33

The jungle was wet and muddy, making the journey difficult for travelers and their mules.

You rest a week before beginning the journey to Panama City. Your mule train follows a narrow, rocky path through a forest of palm trees. For hours, you slog through the jungle. Your mule often loses its footing on loose stones and slips into the mud and muck.

You are filthy when you finally reach the city. Hundreds of people are waiting for boats to San Francisco. You'll have to wait with them.

One morning, you wake with stomach pains. Your mouth and skin are dry.

"Cholera," the doctor says. Your friends force you to drink boiled water, but the disease has already taken hold. You die within a few days. There will be no California gold for you.

THE END

To follow another path, turn to page 11.
To read the conclusion, turn to page 101.

You are stranded for more than a month in Panama City.

On May 6, just before dawn, cannon fire announces the arrival of two ships. Crowds storm the beach. Fistfights break out as passengers argue about who will get to go.

Finally, those in charge hold a drawing. You are given number 179. If your number is called, you'll have a spot on one of the ships. If not, you'll have to wait for another boat.

"348. 22. 287." You're starting to worry. "179." You leap into the air and race to the dock, clutching your number.

The ship is so crowded that you sleep on deck in a makeshift tent. The food is awful, but you are happy to be on your way at last.

You reach San Francisco on June 6, 1849. You are exhausted. Should you rest in San Francisco or go directly to the gold fields?

➤ To rest in San Francisco, turn to page 74.

➤ To go to the gold fields, turn to page 77.

Repairing the sails often meant
climbing the ship's mast.

When you step forward and volunteer
to fix the sail, others cheer.

Ice crystals sting your face as you climb
up the ship's mast. Snow clouds your vision.
You reach out to grasp the jib at the very
moment that a huge wave slams the ship.

The jolt tears you from the rigging. You grab for the sail, but it rips in your hand. You fall into the icy Atlantic, clutching a small piece of sailcloth.

The crew and passengers attempt to rescue you, but it's too dark and stormy. A few friends linger at the rail, shaking their heads over your untimely death.

THE END

To follow another path, turn to page 11.
To read the conclusion, turn to page 101.

39

Travelers loaded their wagons with food, clothing, and other supplies before leaving for California.

CHAPTER 3

WAGONS WEST

An overland trip to California will be the adventure of a lifetime. In February, you see an ad for the Pioneer Line. They are offering a comfortable ride from Independence, Missouri, to California in 55 days. The $200 price includes transportation, food, and space for 100 pounds of baggage for each person.

When you show your father the ad, he shakes his head. "That doesn't make sense. It's almost 1,800 miles from Missouri to California. They'd have to go more than 30 miles a day to get there so quickly. They won't find mules that fast anywhere."

Turn the page.

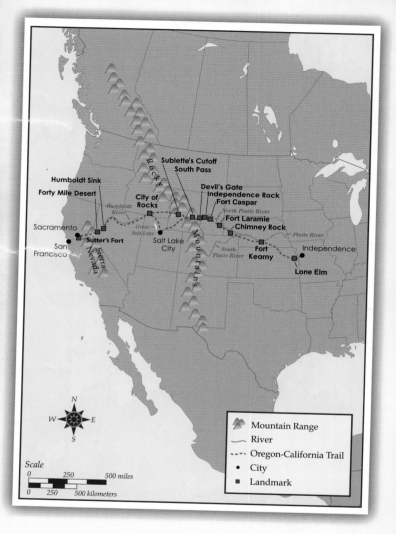

Humboldt Sink

Forty Mile Desert

Sublette's Cutoff
South Pass

City of
Rocks

Devil's Gate
Independence Rock
Fort Caspar

Humboldt River

North Platte River

Sacramento

Sutter's Fort

Fort Laramie
Chimney Rock

Great Salt Lake

Platte River

San
Francisco

Salt Lake
City

South Platte River

Fort
Kearny

Independence

Sierra
Nevada

Lone Elm

Rocky Mountains

N

W   E

S

Scale

0   250   500 miles

0   250   500 kilometers

Mountain Range

River

Oregon-California Trail

City

Landmark

"But the ad says . . ."

"Don't believe everything you read. Join a wagon train. With your own wagon, you can make the decisions about what to bring and how fast to travel."

Wagon trains are slow. The Pioneer Line promises you'll be in California long before the other wagon trains arrive—if the ad is true. Will you take a chance on the Pioneer Line or join a wagon train?

→To take the Pioneer Line, turn to page 44.

→ To join a wagon train, turn to page 47.

When you learn that the men organizing the Pioneer Line are successful businessmen, you relax. Surely they know what they are doing.

You join the Pioneer Line on April 15 near Independence, Missouri. As soon as you arrive, you buy a horse. It will be fun to explore the country on horseback as you travel west.

The Pioneer Line sets off May 15 with 20 wagons for 161 passengers and crew. Another 22 wagons carry supplies or baggage.

It is only days before William Millen and Oliver Trowbridge, two of your fellow travelers, develop cholera and die. You bury them near the camp at Lone Elm before moving on. Soon, several more men have developed cholera.

A few weeks later, you pass Fort Kearny. The Pioneer Line is traveling only about 15 miles a day.

The captain decides that the heavy loads are slowing down the mules. "From now on, only those too ill to walk can ride in the wagons," he says. "We'll dump extra supplies too." Everyone tosses barrels of books, extra clothing, and even food out of the wagons.

Days on the trail are dull. You get up at dawn, break up camp, travel until the mules are worn out, set up camp, and sleep. Then you do it again the next day.

You follow the south bank of the Platte River to the North Platte River. By late June, you spot Chimney Rock on the horizon. You have traveled about one-third of the trail.

Turn the page.

A few weeks later, you reach Fort Caspar, where the North Platte makes a southern turn. At most rivers, the mules can pull the wagons across. But the North Platte is deep and tricky. The captain plans to send the wagons across on the ferry. The ferry carries across one wagon, plus as many people and animals that can fit, at a time. With several wagon trains in line ahead of you, it will be a long, boring wait.

"It's a good day for a swim," one man says.

"The river's a bit rough," you say, noticing tree branches spinning in the muddy water.

"Afraid to get wet?" he asks.

It's a dare. You're a good swimmer. Will you take the dare?

➻ *To wait, turn to page* **58**.

➻ *To take the dare, turn to page* **62**.

You join a group of 60 New England men heading for the gold fields. Everyone pays $600 toward the cost of supplies, wagons, and oxen. When you reach California, you'll divide up the wagons and supplies.

Your horse takes you from Massachusetts to Missouri, where you catch up with the rest of the company. Within a few days, the company has purchased 54 oxen, 18 wagons, 10 milk cows, and four ponies.

"If we leave too early, there won't be enough feed for the oxen. But if we wait too long, there will be snow in the mountains," the leader says. You leave May 15.

Wagon trains stretch ahead of you and behind you. At night, the glow of campfires lights the sky.

Turn the page.

Chimney Rock in Nebraska Territory was an easily recognizable landmark for travelers heading west.

Following the North Platte River, you make your way across the prairie. In June, you spot a thin column of stone on the horizon. "That's Chimney Rock," a man says. Days pass before you actually pass the 300-foot-tall landmark. A few days later, you pass Fort Laramie. About one-third of the trip is complete.

Just past Fort Caspar, the trail crosses the North Platte. At other rivers, the oxen pulled the wagons across the river. But the North Platte is strong and churning with mud. You will have to wait for the ferry.

Hundreds of wagons wait in line ahead of you. You watch as they are loaded and carried across, one by one. To save time and space, some people are having their animals swim across. Some of the animals struggle to stay above water. Every person and animal that swims frees up ferry space and makes the line shorter. You are a good swimmer. Should you wait for the ferry or swim across with your horse?

➻ To go by ferry, turn to page **50**.

➻ To swim, turn to page **62**.

You hear a child yell, "Barky!"

You turn in time to see a large dog jump into the water. It struggles against the wild current and then disappears into the churning waters.

You're glad you waited for the ferry.

Once all the wagons are across the river, your group travels west through dusty and dry land. The few pools of water you find are undrinkable. You count 16 skeletons of cattle most likely killed by drinking bad water.

In early July, you finally see Independence Rock. It rises in the distance like a huge gray whale. Like hundreds of other pioneers, you stop to carve your name on the soft rock. You've been on the California Trail for almost two months, but you're only halfway to California. Dreams of gold keep you going.

Most wagon trains reached Independence Rock around the Fourth of July.

A few miles past Independence Rock is Devil's Gate, a narrow split carved in the rocks by river water. Just beyond that is the South Pass through the Rocky Mountains. You have reached the halfway point.

51

Turn the page.

One night, the captain calls everyone to a meeting. "The trail splits ahead," he explains. "The southern trail leads to Salt Lake City. To the north is Sublette's Cutoff. It's shorter than the route through Salt Lake City."

"Take the shortcut!" shouts one man.

"But if we go to Salt Lake," another man argues, "we can get new supplies and trade our tired oxen for new animals."

"Let's have a vote," the captain decides. "Should we take the trail to Salt Lake City or try Sublette's Cutoff?"

➤ If you vote to go to Salt Lake City, go to page 53.

➤ If you vote to take Sublette's Cutoff, turn to page 55.

It will be good to get new supplies in Salt Lake City. It is the first city you've seen in several months. Adobe brick cottages and log cabins fill the neighborhoods. Vegetables grow in green gardens. Trees line the streets.

As soon as repairs are finished, the wagon train is ready to move on. But several townspeople warn you to wait until spring. "Snow will block the mountains before you can reach California," they say. "You'll be trapped."

The rest of the group ignores the warning. But you're not so sure. You are as eager as anyone else to get to the gold fields, but is it worth risking your life? Will you continue with the wagon train or wait in Salt Lake City until spring?

53

→ To go on, turn to page 54.

→ To stay in Salt Lake City, turn to page 59.

Travelers used ropes to keep their wagons from plunging over sharp mountain cliffs.

You don't want to wait in Salt Lake City. The gold seems closer than ever, and you decide to keep going.

The trail out of Salt Lake City is steep. Men tie ropes to the wagons to keep them from dropping down the cliffs.

One day as you are riding your horse, snow begins to fall.

Turn to page 65.

Sublette's Cutoff may be shorter, but it's a rough trail. For two days, there is no water for the animals. They stumble on. When you get within sight of a small river, the animals perk up. You unhitch them, and they stampede to the water.

In late July, you reach a rocky area called the City of Rocks. Your wagon train winds its way between steep mountain cliffs. Three of the wagons break down, so others agree to carry extra supplies. The remaining wagons groan under the heavy load.

After a few weeks, a group heading east warns, "There's 40 miles of desert ahead. Load the wagons with hay for the animals and fill barrels with water."

Turn the page.

You tie your remaining food and a shovel onto your horse's back and throw the rest of your supplies away. You cut whatever grass you can find, stuff it into the wagon, and fill barrels with boiled water.

"We'll travel by night and sleep in the heat of the day," the captain says.

It's dark when you start across the Forty Mile Desert. Moonlight shows the bodies of dead animals and abandoned wagons beside the trail. Moving through sand is difficult. The animals refuse to move until you hold grass in front of their noses and coax them forward.

It takes two nights and one day to cross the desert. Water runs out just before dawn . . . but you've made it! The desert is behind you.

There's one last mountain range to climb. When you finally reach Emigrant Gap, you lower the remaining wagons on ropes to the last valley. At long last, you're in California!

Before the company breaks up, you split the remaining supplies. One man offers you a blanket and pickax in exchange for your horse. You hate to give up your horse, but you need the supplies.

You're eager to start digging, but it would be nice to have a meal in Sacramento, the nearest town, and catch up on the latest news.

57

→ *To go to Sacramento, turn to page **75**.*

→ *To start digging, turn to page **77**.*

You watch from the bank as the man who dared you to swim gets tangled in a tree branch. "Help! Help!"

You wade in and free him.

"I was foolish to try," he says. "Getting to California and the gold is what really matters. I have a new bride waiting for me back home. My gold will buy us a farm."

The country beyond the river is rocky and dry. Wind and dust are your constant companions. You pass dead oxen and broken wagons along the trail. You see stoves, farm equipment, and even mining tools that were tossed from overloaded wagons.

Turn to page 60.

You find work in Salt Lake City at a stable. Many wagon trains stop there to trade tired animals for fresh ones. You sleep in a room at the back of the stable and eat your meals with the stable owner, his wife, and their four daughters.

The oldest daughter, Helen, is clever and beautiful. She makes you laugh. Over the winter, you fall in love. When spring comes, you are torn between your love for Helen and your desire for riches.

You are so close to the gold fields. If you don't go, you'll never know if you could have struck it rich. What do you do?

→ To leave Helen and go to the gold fields, turn to page **68**.

→ To stay in Salt Lake City, turn to page **66**.

Evening camps gave travelers a chance to relax and trade stories with one another.

After almost two months on the trail, you reach the South Pass. Everyone is tired and complaining. "These mosquitoes are as big as turkeys," a man says, slapping his arm.

"They're no bigger than crows," you joke.

"Are we almost to California?" someone asks.

Another man laughs. "We're only halfway there. And the worst is yet to come."

Several wagon trains camp near you in the evening. One night, a man from another group says, "We expected the fast wagons of the Pioneer Line to rush past us."

"They haven't kept their promises," you say.

After the South Pass, you reach the City of Rocks, where stone towers stretch to the sky. Then you follow the Humboldt River. The Forty Mile Desert lies ahead.

Some of your friends have scurvy, a disease caused by lack of vitamin C. They are weak, their gums bleed, and they may die. If you stay with them, you may be delayed weeks.

Four men have decided to go on ahead. Will you go with them?

→ To stay with the Pioneer Line, turn to page 63.

→ To go on ahead, turn to page 67.

You jump into the river. Brrr! It's freezing. Oxen, mules, horses, and cows from various wagon trains struggle to cross the river against the strong currents.

You are halfway across when a tree limb rushes toward you. You try to avoid it, but your shirt gets tangled in the branches. It pulls you deep into the muddy river. You fight, but you can't get free.

No one notices you are missing until evening, when you fail to show up for supper. "Drowned," they decide. They say a prayer before moving on.

THE END

To follow another path, turn to page 11.
To read the conclusion, turn to page 101.

You may have to wait a few extra weeks before getting rich, but staying with your sick friends feels like the right thing to do. You struggle across the desert, traveling at night, resting by day. After two terrible nights, you reach the end of the desert, feeling more dead than alive.

The journey is not over. You still have to cross the Sierra Nevada mountain range. You gather your strength and courage.

Turn the page.

Paths through the mountain
ranges were narrow and tricky.

As you climb to the first mountain summit,
snow begins to fall. The captain fears the sick
men won't survive the storm. "You go ahead on
your horse," he says. "We'll follow as soon as
the weather clears."

As you ride ahead, the storm worsens.
Soon, you can't see where you are going.
Is this the trail?

With a snort, your horse stops. He refuses to go any farther. You climb down and tug on his halter, but he still won't budge. You pull harder. With a snap, the leather breaks and you tumble off a cliff.

No one will ever find your frozen body. Your parents will spend their lives wondering what became of you and your golden dreams.

65

THE END

To follow another path, turn to page 11.
To read the conclusion, turn to page 101.

Helen is worth more than all the riches in California. You stay in Salt Lake City and ask Helen's father for permission to marry her.

"What about California and the gold?" he asks.

"I don't really care about that anymore," you say.

You marry Helen and look forward to a happy life in Salt Lake City.

THE END

To follow another path, turn to page 11.
To read the conclusion, turn to page 101.

Going on ahead is the wise choice. You leave your horse behind for one of the sick men to ride. You'll walk the rest of the way.

You push across the sandy desert and begin the climb into the Sierra Nevada range. The trail is packed with people trying to get to California before winter sets in.

On September 21, 1849, you reach California. The journey that was supposed to take 55 days took 129.

67

Turn to page 69.

Saying good-bye to Helen is not easy, but you've traveled too far to give up now. You leave Salt Lake City with another wagon train and travel north past Great Salt Lake until you reach the City of Rocks.

From there, you follow the Humboldt River from its source to a swampy area called Humboldt Sink. After Humboldt Sink, you must cross the Forty Mile Desert. You gather extra water and food for the animals, but leave behind just about everything else. Two long days later, you reach the western side of the desert. In only a few more weeks, you reach the mining town of Weaverville, near Sutter's Fort. California gold at last!

Everywhere you look, people are searching for gold. It's tempting to start digging. But first you need supplies. You could try to buy them here and now. But the prices are high. Maybe it would be cheaper to go to Sacramento and buy your supplies there. Or is it worth paying extra for supplies so you can start digging sooner?

➼ To stay and buy supplies, turn to page 82.

➼ To go to Sacramento, turn to page 75.

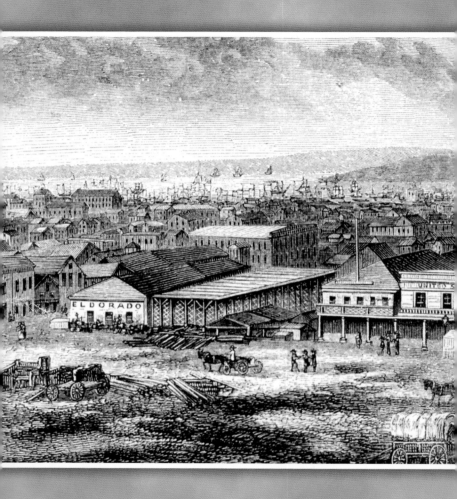

During the gold rush, Portsmouth Square in San Francisco was the center of many town events and activities.

CHAPTER 4

CALIFORNIA!

You take a room at the Parker House Hotel and wait to hear from the men who are selling the cargo. It may be a while before they contact you.

As you leave the hotel for an evening stroll, a man says, "Look!"

Gold sparkles in the street.

You laugh. "Is it that easy to find gold?"

"I wish it were. That's just dust from a miner's boot. Maybe tomorrow it will be dust from mine."

"Yours and mine, too," you say.

Turn the page.

You glimpse a tent with a sign that says, "Eat." Inside, men sit at long tables. Near the entrance, a woman is cooking. "Five dollars," she says, and hands you a plate of beans, cornbread, and coffee.

Back at the hotel, a message from your company is waiting for you: *Meet at Portsmouth Square Bank. Noon tomorrow.*

At the bank, you hear good news. The cargo sold quickly. Your share is $800. That's a $200 profit!

As you leave the bank, the owner asks if anyone would like a job. "I pay well. There's far more money in banking gold than there is in digging it. If that weren't true, I'd be living in a tent panning for gold."

Most of the men shake their heads. You hesitate. The miners you've seen are rough gambling men who tell stories of gunfights at the mines. Others dig for weeks without success. Do you really want to dig in the fields when you could live well in the city? At the same time, you came here for adventure. Will a banking job have the excitement you crave?

→ *To go to the gold fields, turn to page* **77**.

→ *To take the bank job, turn to page* **86**.

The only hotel you can find in San Francisco is a tent. You feel better after a good rest and healthy food. You book passage on a small boat going up the crooked Sacramento River.

A week later, you reach Sacramento. It will be another short journey to the gold fields. Will you go directly to the fields or stay in Sacramento to rest a while?

➤ If you remain in Sacramento, go to page 75.

➤ To go directly to the gold fields, turn to page 77.

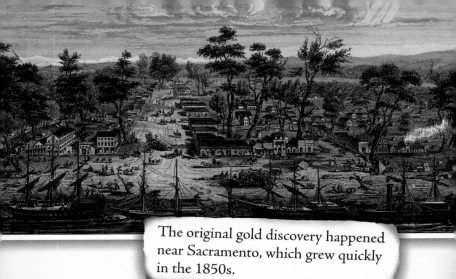

The original gold discovery happened near Sacramento, which grew quickly in the 1850s.

Sacramento is a lively town built almost entirely of tents. Even most hotels, stores, and restaurants are made of cloth. You wander into a pub and talk to some of the miners. They are all discouraged.

"I'm heading home," one says. "There's no gold for me."

"Rents are high. It costs $25 a week just for food. I'm losing money every day I stay."

Turn the page.

Next you step into a store to buy supplies. The man behind the counter asks if you just arrived. You nod.

"Don't even bother going to the fields, kid," he says. "You want to know where the real gold mine is? It's this store right here."

The man watches you as you continue shopping. "I like you. Want a job?" he asks.

You're surprised by the offer and not sure how to respond. You feel like you should give mining a fair shot, but you think of the discouraged miners you met earlier. Maybe this job would be an easier way to get rich.

"It's your choice, of course, but I sure could use the help," the storekeeper says.

→ To go to the gold fields, go to page 77.
→ To take the job in the store, turn to page 80.

You came here to dig for gold, so that's what you'll do. You make your way to a mining camp on the Sacramento River.

Men dig at the river's edge for gold. Others stand in the water, shaking pans. It's called panning. They fill the pan with water and shake it. Any gold hiding in the sand settles into the bottom of the pan.

One group is working with a wooden machine. The bottom part looks like a dugout canoe, but there's a box on top with a metal screen.

"How does that work?" you ask.

Turn the page.

"That top part of the rocker is called the hopper. You shovel rocks, dirt, and sand into it. Then you pour water onto it and shake it."

The man continues. "Gold is heavier than sand, so the water washes away the sand. The gold stays behind. Every so often, we dump the rocks out of the hopper. What's left in the rocker is pure gold dust." All around, you hear the rattle of rocks in the rockers.

Miners used rockers to separate gold dust from sand and rocks.

"Have you found much?" you ask.

"More than $30 worth yesterday," he says. "It would take me more than a month to make that much back home."

He points at the two men next to him in the river. "These fellows are heading over to Dead Man's Hollow tomorrow. They think there's a big vein of gold there. But I'll make my fortune right here."

Should you stay where you are or keep looking for an even richer strike?

79

→ To stay on at the first camp, turn to page 82.

→ To go to Dead Man's Hollow, turn to page 84.

You enjoy working in the store. The owner, Sam Brannan, owns several stores in the area. "Back when James Marshall found those first bits of gold, I got an idea," he tells you. "I bought all the pans, pickaxes, and shovels in town. Then I got some gold dust and ran through the streets, shouting, 'Gold! Gold from the American River!' I got everybody excited about the gold. They had to come to my store to buy the mining equipment, and I raised the prices."

The plan made Brannan one of California's first millionaires. He began buying land and opening more stores.

After a few years, you earn enough money to open your own store. Others may find gold in the fields, but you will make your fortune as a storekeeper.

THE END

To follow another path, turn to page 11.
To read the conclusion, turn to page 101.

As you walk among the gold fields, you buy a pickax for $6.50. You find a little gold: 50 cents worth on Monday, $1 on Tuesday, and $1.70 on Wednesday. On Thursday, you do better: $20. Each day, you seem to do a little better. Maybe tomorrow, you'll strike it rich.

You buy a supper of beans and bacon. You feel ill and wonder if you have a touch of scurvy, a sickness caused by not eating enough fresh fruits and vegetables. It's hard to get healthy food at the diggings. Maybe all you need is rest.

But by morning you are feeling worse, and you have a bad cough. You dream about sleeping in a warm bed and slurping your mother's soup. But your bed is damp and cold, and your mother is far away.

You keep on working, even though you feel terrible. One sunny morning, you finally notice a flash of gold. When you reach down to pick it up, you collapse.

"Help!" you whimper.

Other miners carry you back to your bed. You lay under your blankets, shivering and coughing. Two days later, you die of a lung infection called pneumonia, never having struck it rich.

THE END

To follow another path, turn to page 11.
To read the conclusion, turn to page 101.

"They call it Dead Man's Hollow because two men were murdered here last summer for their gold," another miner says.

It's raining when you arrive. You set to work building a small cabin with a fireplace. You dig by day and visit with nearby miners at night. Despite the rumors of riches, no one has found any big gold nuggets yet. You find a dollar or two a day in gold dust, but spend more than that on bacon.

Miners became discouraged after days of mining without striking gold.

You are homesick and discouraged.

You visit the mines at Weaverville, Hangtown, Georgetown, and Sutter's Mill where gold was first discovered. "This is where the gold rush started," someone says.

"Maybe this is where it ends for me," you say.

"Don't give up yet. There's plenty of gold. It could be just over the next hill."

Do you try one more time to strike it rich, or do you go home while you still can?

To try one more time, turn to page **88**.

To go home, turn to page **93**.

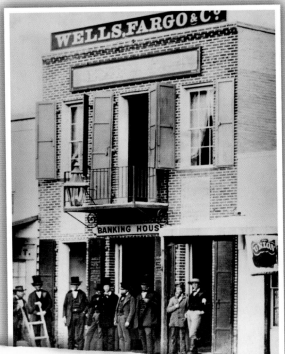

Wells Fargo and Company opened their first San Francisco bank in 1852.

You enjoy your work at the bank. Every day you see gold, but you never have to lift a shovel. San Francisco is growing, and with new stores, restaurants, and hotels, there's a great future for a banker.

You write home and tell your family that you'll be staying in San Francisco. You also send a money order to your father to repay your passage. "Come visit," you write, although you know it will be years before they do. Someday there will be a train all the way from Boston to San Francisco. Then they'll come. California is changing, and you want to play a role in its future.

THE END

To follow another path, turn to page 11.
To read the conclusion, turn to page 101.

You decide to give yourself one more chance to strike gold.

You move to an isolated area in the hills and begin digging about 20 feet from a small stream. Someone else has begun digging here, but the claim looks abandoned.

One day, you make $5. Another day, you make $20. "Better and better," you say.

The next day, you have some good luck. "Gold!" you yell, and pry out a large nugget. It weighs almost 5 pounds. It must be worth more than $1,000!

You don't even see the other man until he speaks. "What you got there?" he asks.

Some miners moved from claim to claim in search of better luck and more gold.

The man looks hungry and tired. You have a bad feeling about him. Should you tell him what you have found or try to hide the nugget?

❧ To hide the nugget, turn to page **90**.

❧ To tell the man, turn to page **91**.

You bend down and slip the nugget into your pack before he can see.

"I found $20 worth of gold dust yesterday," you say. It's not a lie, but it's not the whole truth either.

"I've been digging in this spot for weeks now without finding a thing. You take over the claim if you want. I'm giving up. It's useless. I sold my farm to pay for my trip to California. Now I've got nothing."

This man is no thief. He's just a tired miner. Is it your fault he gave up before finding the gold? You feel guilty not telling him the truth. But if you don't tell, you can keep all the gold for yourself.

➤ To tell him about the nugget, turn to page **91**.

➤ To keep the secret, turn to page **94**.

"Your luck is about to change," you say. "Your claim is finally paying off." You hold out the large nugget.

"It's a doozy," he says. "By rights, it belongs to you. I'd already given up."

"I could use a hand," you say and offer to split the profits.

Miner William Stewart poses with a pan of gold in 1850.

Turn the page.

Together, you continue to find gold. Two weeks later, when the strike seems to run out, you have over $20,000 each.

"I'm going home to my wife and children," your partner says with a smile.

"I'll either go home to Massachusetts or start a business here in California. A man could make a fortune here."

Your partner laughs. "You already did."

→ *To go home, turn to page* **96**.

→ *To stay in California, turn to page* **97**.

You save whatever money you can during the winter, then sell your supplies and join a company heading east. In your last months in California, you collect stories about the gold rush. It is all you have to take home.

THE END

To follow another path, turn to page 11.
To read the conclusion, turn to page 101.

Miners often worked their claims by themselves.

"Good luck," the discouraged miner says as he leaves.

"Safe travels," you say.

You keep the nugget in your pack and return to digging. It's a rich vein. Soon you have a pile of apple-sized nuggets.

It's nearly dark when three strangers approach you.

"The gold or your life," the leader says.

You reach for the gold.

"He's going for a gun," the leader yells. His partners open fire. They take the gold and run, leaving you for dead in the diggings.

THE END

To follow another path, turn to page 11.
To read the conclusion, turn to page 101.

California may be beautiful, but Massachusetts is where you plan to spend your life.

The whole town greets you on your return. Your mother hugs you, your father shakes your hand, and your brothers and sisters ask if you brought them any gold.

You sprinkle a little gold dust into their hands. "My treasure is right here," you say. "I've had enough adventures to last a lifetime."

THE END

To follow another path, turn to page 11.
To read the conclusion, turn to page 101.

You settle in San Francisco. It's a booming city with lots of opportunity. First you buy a large riverboat to bring people from San Francisco to Sacramento. Then you invest in a stagecoach line that runs throughout the state of California.

In 1860, a wealthy businessman named Charles Crocker begins to talk about building a railroad through the Sierra Nevada range. Along with Mark Hopkins, Collis Huntington, and Leland Stanford, he forms the Central Pacific railroad. You decide to put your money into the railroad too. You grow richer and richer. People call you a gold rush millionaire.

Turn the page.

Sam Brannan was a wealthy businessman, but he quickly lost everything and died penniless.

Your luck was not just in finding gold, but also in using it wisely. You know others who made money in the gold rush and lost it gambling or investing poorly. You think especially of Sam Brannan, one of California's first millionaires. He made poor decisions, leaving him broke and homeless before his death. You are determined not to follow in his footsteps.

THE END

To follow another path, turn to page 11.
To read the conclusion, turn to page 101.

James Marshall's discovery of gold set off the gold rush.

CHAPTER 5

THE PATH TO RICHES

The golden sparkle that caught James Marshall's eye at John Sutter's Mill on January 24, 1848, sparked a bout of gold fever that gripped the world. He and Sutter tried to keep quiet about their discovery. But news of the gold leaked out slowly, first to San Francisco and then to areas within sailing distance—Oregon, Mexico, Hawaii, Chile, and Peru. In August 1848, the *New York Herald* published the news. People poured into California from all over. The gold rush was on.

In 1849, records show that at least 19,718 gold seekers traveled to California by sea. At least another 22,500 people traveled overland the same year. These people were known as 49ers.

It was not an easy trip. Going around Cape Horn was the safest choice. In 1849, there were fewer than 50 deaths along the Cape Horn route. Going across Panama was more dangerous because of cholera, a disease we now know is caused by drinking bad water. Overland travelers faced many dangers, including cholera and other diseases, starvation, and accidents.

The gold rush brought thousands of people to California in 1849.

Digging for gold wasn't the only path to riches in California. Some people made money selling supplies to the miners. Others worked as carpenters, mechanics, and clerks in the booming cities of San Francisco and Sacramento. They built homes, opened stores, and ran hotels. There were jobs for teachers, doctors, lawyers, and restaurant and hotel managers.

The gold rush was over almost as quickly as it began. In 1852, gold was discovered in Australia. The next year, more gold was found in British Columbia. Many California miners moved on to these new sites, unable to resist the dream of instant riches. But the California they left behind was forever changed. It had grown from a distant frontier to one of the richest places in America.

The population of San Francisco hit 25,000 after 1850.

TIME LINE

January 24, 1848—James Marshall discovers pea-sized nuggets of gold at Sutter's Mill.

February 2, 1848—The United States and Mexico sign the Treaty of Guadalupe Hidalgo, selling California and other areas to the United States.

March 15, 1848—A small article in *The Californian*, a San Francisco newspaper, reports the discovery of gold. Many people do not believe the story.

May 12, 1848—Storekeeper Sam Brannan sets off gold fever in San Francisco by waving a bottle of gold dust while yelling "Gold! Gold!" in the city's streets. He received the gold as payment for goods in his store.

August 19, 1848—The *New York Herald* newspaper prints an article about the gold discovery; it becomes world news.

December 5, 1848—President James K. Polk confirms the gold discovery in his annual speech to Congress.

February 28, 1849—Steamship service begins from Panama to California.

April 1849—The first wagon trains leave Missouri for California.

October 1849—Large numbers of Europeans begin to sail to California.

March 27, 1850—Thadeus Hildreth finds a 22-pound gold nugget near the town of Columbia, California. The population of the town explodes to 15,000.

September 9, 1850—California becomes the 31st state.

1852—Many miners leave California for gold discoveries in Australia.

1853—Many more California miners leave for new gold discoveries in British Columbia.

1854—A 195-pound chunk of gold is found at Carson Hill in Calaveras County. It is the largest piece of gold known to have been found in California.

1889—Sam Brannan, one of California's first millionaires, dies.

OTHER PATHS TO EXPLORE

In this book, you've seen how the events surrounding the gold rush look different from several points of view.

Perspectives on history are as varied as the people who lived it. You can explore other paths on your own to learn more about what happened. Seeing history from many points of view is an important part of understanding it.

Here are some ideas for other gold rush points of view to explore:

* Many gold seekers left their families at home when they headed west. What would it have been like to be a wife or child left behind?

* Americans weren't the only people who rushed to California in 1849. Many people sailed from other countries, such as Chile, Peru, or China. How were these groups treated by the other miners?

* During the gold rush, only about 10 percent of people living in California were women. What was life like for them?

READ MORE

Aretha, David. *The Gold Rush to California's Riches.* The Wild History of the American West. Berkeley Heights, N.J.: MyReportLinks.com Books, 2006.

Doeden, Matt. *John Sutter and the California Gold Rush.* Graphic Library. Graphic History. Mankato, Minn.: Capstone Press, 2006.

Mason, Paul. *Panning for Gold.* Chicago: Raintree, 2007.

Somervill, Barbara A. *The Gold Rush: Buried Treasure.* Trailblazers of the West. New York: Children's Press, 2005.

INTERNET SITES

FactHound offers a safe, fun way to find Internet sites related to this book. All of the sites on FactHound have been researched by our staff.

Here's how:
1. Visit *www.facthound.com*
2. Choose your grade level.
3. Type in this book ID **1429601604** for age-appropriate sites. You may also browse subjects by clicking on letters, or by clicking on pictures and words.
4. Click on the **Fetch It** button.

FactHound will fetch the best sites for you!

Glossary

bungo (BUN-goh)—a large dugout canoe

cholera (KOL-ur-uh)—a disease that causes sickness and diarrhea

claim (KLAYM)—a piece of land for which a miner has declared a right to occupy and search for valuable minerals

current (KUR-uhnt)—the fastest-flowing part of a river or stream

lobscouse (LOB-skows)—a sailor's dish prepared by stewing or baking bits of meat with vegetables, hardtack, and other ingredients

pneumonia (noo-MOH-nyuh)—a serious disease that causes the lungs to become inflamed and filled with a thick fluid that makes breathing difficult

rocker (ROK-ur)— a rocking device used by miners to wash out gold from dirt and sand by hand; a rocker is sometimes called a cradle.

scurvy (SKUR-vee)—a deadly disease caused by lack of vitamin C; scurvy produces swollen limbs, bleeding gums, and weakness.

suet (SOO-it)—a hard fat from cattle and sheep that is used in cooking

BIBLIOGRAPHY

Brands, H. W. *The Age of Gold: The California Gold Rush and the New American Dream.* New York: Doubleday, 2002.

Delgado, James P. *To California by Sea: A Maritime History of the California Gold Rush.* Studies in Maritime History. Columbia, S.C.: University of South Carolina Press, 1990.

Gordon, Mary McDougall, ed. *Overland to California with the Pioneer Line: The Gold Rush Diary of Bernard J. Reid.* Urbana, Ill.: University of Illinois Press, 1987.

Holliday, J. S. *The World Rushed In: The California Gold Rush Experience.* New York: Simon and Schuster, 1981.

Pomfret, John Edwin, ed. *California Gold Rush Voyages, 1848–1849: Three Original Narratives.* San Marino, Calif.: Huntington Library, 1954.

Rohrbough, Malcolm J. *Days of Gold: The California Gold Rush and the American Nation.* Berkeley: University of California Press, 1997.

Walker, Dale L. *Eldorado: The California Gold Rush.* New York: Forge, 2003.

INDEX